Cover: Nathan Love

mheducation.com/prek-12

Send all inquiries to:
McGraw-Hill Education
Two Penn Plaza
New York, New York 10121

ISBN: 978-0-07-901812-0
MHID: 0-07-901812-2

Printed in the United States of America.

4 5 6 7 8 9 QVS 23 22 21 20 19

D

Program Authors

Diane August

Donald R. Bear

Kathy R. Bumgardner

Jana Echevarria

Douglas Fisher

David J. Francis

Vicki Gibson

Jan Hasbrouck

Timothy Shanahan

Josefina V. Tinajero

Mc
Graw
Hill
Education

Animals Everywhere

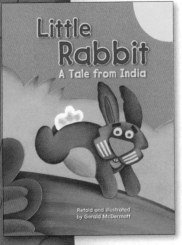

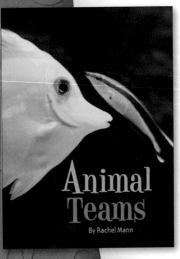

my.mheducation.com

(b) The Gorilla Foundation

5

UNIT 5

Figure It Out

my.mheducation.com

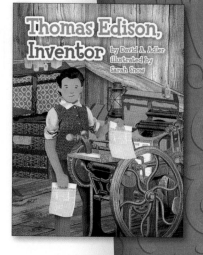

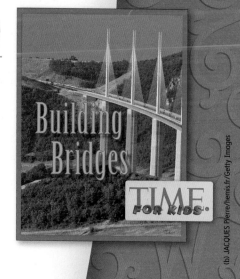
7

UNIT 6

Together We Can!

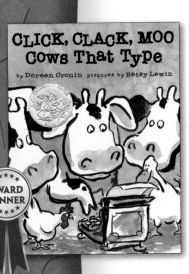

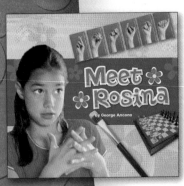

my.mheducation.com

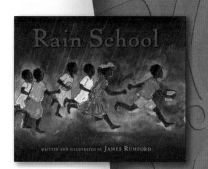

Genre Folktale

Essential Question

How do animals' bodies help them?

Read about how a little rabbit runs from a falling forest.

Little Rabbit
A Tale from India

Retold and illustrated
by Gerald McDermott

One day, Little Rabbit lay under a tree.

The day was **splendid** and he felt good.

Then he began to think.

"What if the forest falls? What will happen to me?"

Just then, something fell past his head.

It landed with a big thump!

Little Rabbit jumped up. "The forest is falling!"
he yelled.

"I cannot stay! I must be on my way!"

14

He hopped and hopped using his long back legs. His white tail flapped up and down.

He passed Fox. "Why are you hopping so fast?" asked Fox.

"The forest is falling!" yelled Little Rabbit. "You cannot stay. Come quick. Let's be on **our** way!"

"Wait for me!" yelled Fox.

He ran and ran. His red tail swayed this way and that.

Deer heard **eight** legs run past.

16

"Why are you running so fast?" asked Deer.

"The forest is falling!" yelled Fox. "You cannot stay. Come quick! We must be on our way!"

"Wait for me!" yelled Deer. With her long, slim legs, Deer ran fast.

The **animals** ran in a line. They passed an Ox.

"Can I play?" asked Ox.

"It is not a game" said Deer. "The forest is falling! You cannot stay! Come quick. We must be on our way."

"I am big and wide. I cannot run fast," sobbed Ox.

"We will wait," said Deer.

Ox thumped and clumped behind the rest.

The animals ran on and on.

They woke Tiger up.

"What is going on?" yelled Tiger.

"The forest is falling!" said Ox. "You cannot stay. Come quick. We must be on our way!"

"Wait for me!" said Tiger.

They passed an Elephant.

"The forest is falling," yelled Tiger. "You cannot stay. Come quick. We must be on our way!"

"Wait for me!" yelled Elephant.

She had legs as thick as tree trunks.

Stomp! Stomp!

When she ran, the whole forest shook.

21

The animals ran on and on.

"Run away! Run away!" they yelled.

They passed Lion.

"Stop!" he said. "Can someone tell me what this fuss is **about**?"

"The forest is falling!" explained Elephant. "We are all running away."

Lion stood still and spoke.

"That cannot be true," he said.
"Who told you that?"

"Tiger did," said Elephant.

"Ox did," said Tiger.

"Deer did," said Ox.

"Fox did," said Deer.

"Little Rabbit did," said Fox.

24

Lion looked down at Little Rabbit.

"Well," said Little Rabbit, "I was sitting under a tree and heard a big thump."

"May I visit this place?" said Lion. "I will **give** you a ride."

Little Rabbit let Lion **carry** him. He felt **special**.

All of the animals got to the tree.

"Look," said Lion. "It is just a banana that made that big thump. Next time, don't panic."

"Thank you. I will do as you say," said Little Rabbit.

The animals all lay down to rest.

Little Rabbit stretched his legs. He felt good.

Then he began to think. . . .

About the Author

Gerald McDermott says, "Animals, animals, animals! I love to draw them jumping and hopping and flying across the pages of my books. You can draw animals, too!" Gerald McDermott has illustrated folktales starring interesting animals from all over the world.

Author's Purpose

Gerald McDermott wanted to retell an old folktale. Think of a story about an animal. Draw the animal in your story. Write about it.

Respond to the Text

Retell

Use your own words to retell *Little Rabbit* in order.

First
↓
Next
↓
Then
↓
Last

Write

How do the animals come to believe Little Rabbit's story? Use these sentence starters:

At first, Fox tells. . .

Next, Deer tells. . .

Last, Lion asks. . .

Make Connections

COLLABORATE

Think of an animal you know. How could it use its body to escape danger? ESSENTIAL QUESTION

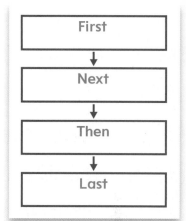

Compare Texts

Read about how fast some animals can move.

Animals Can Go Fast!

What moves at top speed? A plane? A train? How about a bird, a fish, or even a big cat? Many animals move fast. They want to catch other animals or run from danger.

What helps them go fast? Let's find out!

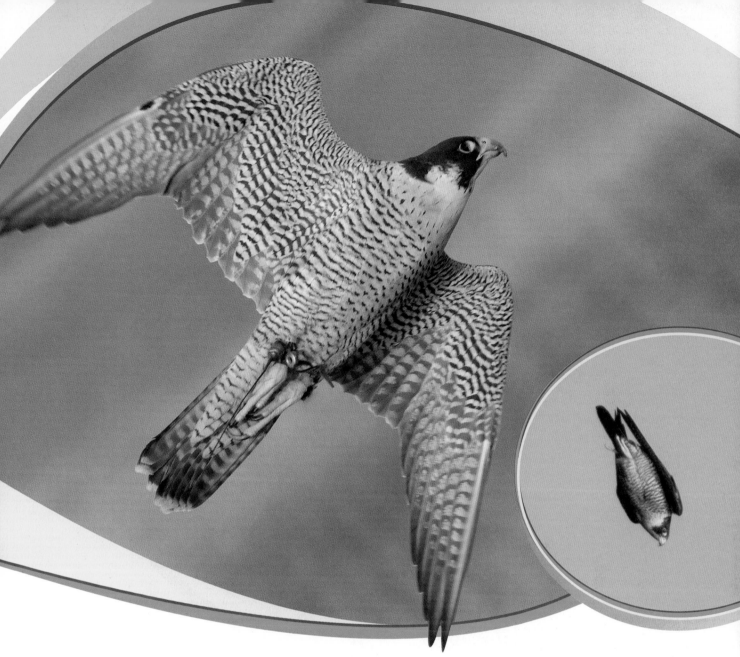

Look up! It's the peregrine falcon! This big bird looks for small birds to eat. When it spots one, it flaps its huge wings to gain speed. Then it tucks its wings and tail to dive. It can go 200 miles an hour like this. That's as fast as a plane!

What cat can run faster than a moving bus? A cheetah chasing a meal. This big cat has a thin body and long legs that help it run fast. Its long tail helps it **balance**. It also uses its tail to steer. It can run 70 miles an hour.

Is that a sailboat in the water? No, it's a sailfish! The fin on its back looks like a sail. When a hungry shark is close, the sailfish folds its fin. Then it jumps out of the sea to **escape**. This fish can jump fast – up to 68 miles an hour. That's faster than a speeding truck.

Hip, hop! Is that a pet rabbit? No, it's a brown hare! It has long hind legs that help it run and hop fast. It zigzags as it runs to trick its hunters. This hare can go 45 miles an hour. That's a lot faster than your pet bunny!

Look at the chart. What does it tell about fast animals? What other fast animals do you know?

ANIMAL	WHAT HELPS THEM GO FAST	HOW FAST THEY GO
Peregrine falcon	Wings, body shape	200 miles an hour
Cheetah	Long thin body, long legs, long tail	70 miles an hour
Sailfish	Foldable fin	68 miles an hour
Brown hare	Long hind legs	45 miles an hour

Make Connections

How does the ability to move fast help animals? **Essential Question**

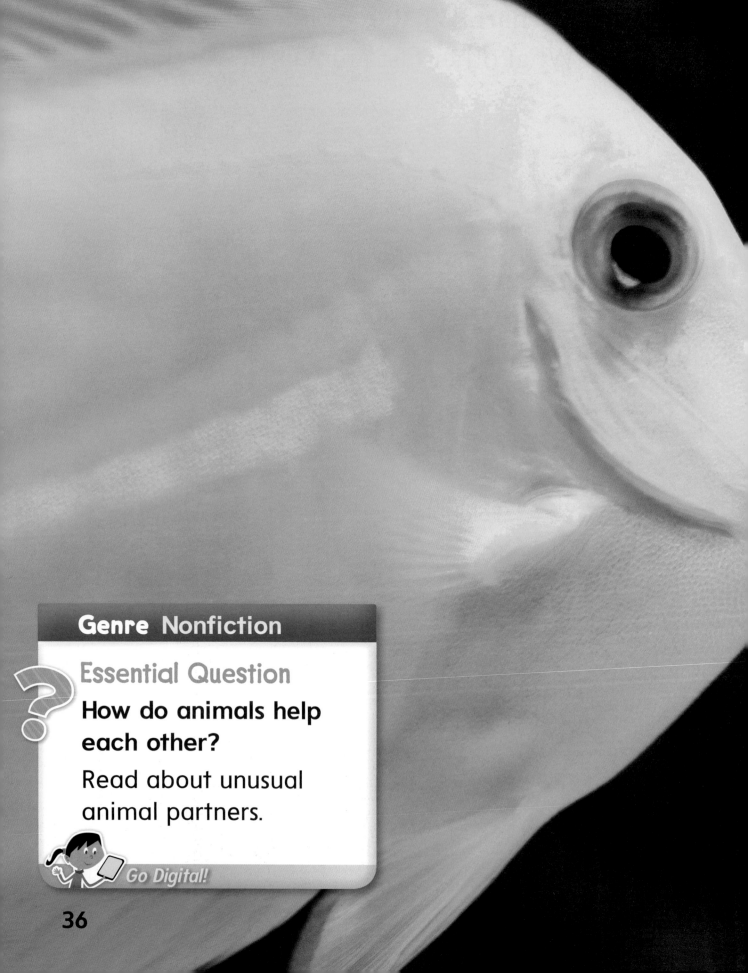

Genre Nonfiction

Essential Question

How do animals help each other?

Read about unusual animal partners.

Go Digital!

Animal Teams

by Rachel Mann

Can a **small** bird help a big giraffe?
Can a shrimp help a fish?

Yes, they can!

These may seem like odd friends. But many animals work together in teams. These animals help each **other** in lots of ways. Let's find out how.

Some birds live off the backs of big animals. Why do the animals let the birds stay? The birds help. They eat bugs off the animals' skin.

The big animals help
the birds, too. They
keep the birds safe.
And it is a good deal
for them **because** they
have lots of sweet bugs
to eat!

The goby fish and the blind shrimp make a good team.

The shrimp can't see, so the goby helps. The goby looks out for **danger**, and the shrimp stays close. When the goby flicks its tail, it means that it is time to hide.

The shrimp helps the goby, too. It will go **into** a hole to hide. It lets the goby hide here, too. The shrimp and the goby hide until it is safe to go out.

43

Zebras and wildebeests live on the hot plains. They both like to eat grass all day.

These animals are seen together a lot. Why?

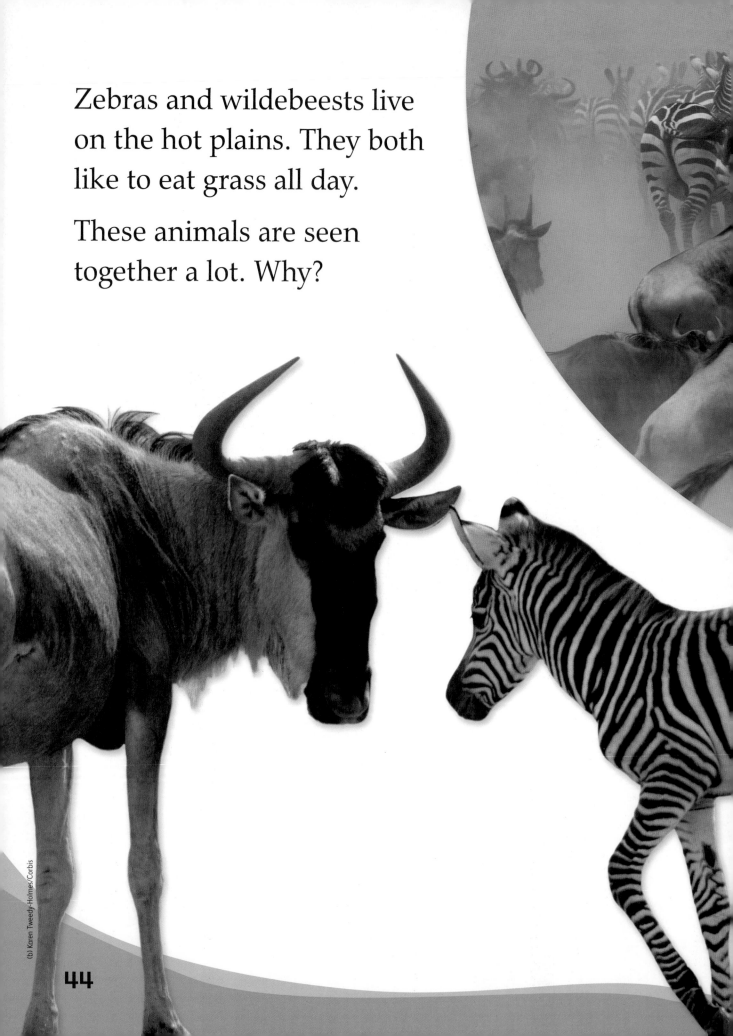

They stay together because they can help each other find fresh grass to eat.

They also help each other keep safe. If a zebra **or** a wildebeest spots danger, it runs. This tells the rest to run, too.

Many fish want to eat the little clown fish. It needs a safe home. So it lives in a sea anemone.

The clown fish is safe because most fish stay away. Why? The sea anemone stings! But the clown fish can not feel its sting.

The clown fish helps its **partner**, too. It swims in and out, in and out. It chases away big fish that could hurt its pal.

A caterpillar needs to be safe so that it can grow.

Who will help? Ants will! Ants see the caterpillar and take it to a safe place.

Why do ants do this?

The caterpillar has a sweet liquid on its skin. The ants like the taste.

Soon the caterpillar will be a pretty **blue** butterfly.

When a little cleaner fish
wants to eat, it looks for
bigger fish to clean. Why?
It gets a free meal when
it cleans.

A cleaner fish eats the
pests off of other fish.

The big fish want to be cleaned! They line up and wait for the cleaner fish to get to them.

One is big, and one is small.
But the two are a team.

When animals team up, they do
what is best for both of them.

Meet the Author

Rachel Mann loves learning about animals, especially animals who act in unexpected ways. She really enjoyed researching and writing *Animal Teams,* because she learned that animals help and need each other just as people do.

Author's Purpose

Rachel Mann wanted to write about animals who do interesting things. Write about an animal that does something you find interesting.

Respond to the Text

Retell

Use your own words to retell the important details in *Animal Teams.*

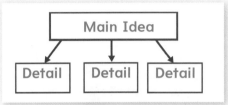

Write

Which animal team do you think is the most interesting? Why? Use these sentence starters:

> The most interesting animal team is...
> They are interesting because...
> The animals help each other when...

Make Connections

COLLABORATE

What animals have you seen together? How did they help each other?

ESSENTIAL QUESTION

55

Busy As a Bee

Bees can make a hive in a tree.

Bees are at home in a hive. All of them have jobs that help the hive.

Worker bees make wax cups called honeycombs.

Lots of **worker** bees help make **honey**.
They help keep the hive clean, too.

Every hive has a **queen** bee. She lays all the eggs.

A hive has drone bees, too. A drone's job is to help the queen make eggs.

A queen bee is with her drones in the hive.

The queen lays eggs inside wax cups.

Papilio/Alamy

New bees hatch from these eggs.
Worker bees feed them.

A big hive is a busy place!

Make Connections

How are the bees like the animals in *Animal Teams*? **Essential Question**

Essential Question

How do animals survive in nature?

Read about how a very unusual animal gets its food.

 Go Digital!

VULTURE VIEW written by April Pulley Sayre, illustrated by Steven Jenkins. Text © 2007 by April Pulley Sayre. Illustrations © 2007 by Steven Jenkins. Used by arrangement with Henry Holt and Company, LLC.

Vulture View

by April Pulley Sayre

illustrated by Steve Jenkins

The sun is rising.
Up, up.
It heats the air.
Up, up.

Wings stretch wide
to catch a ride
on **warming** air.
Going where?

Up, up!
Turkey vultures tilt, soar, scan
to **find** the **food** that vultures can. . .

. . . eat!

That snake **over** there?
No, no.

That fox over there?
No, no.

That bear over there?
No, no.

Vultures smell the air.
They sniff, search, seek
for foods that . . .

. . . REEK!

73

Those fragrant flowers?
No, no.

That spicy smoke?
No, no.

That stinky dead deer?
Yes, yes!

75

Vultures like a mess.
They land and dine.
Rotten is fine.

They eat, then clean.
Splash! Dry. Preen.

79

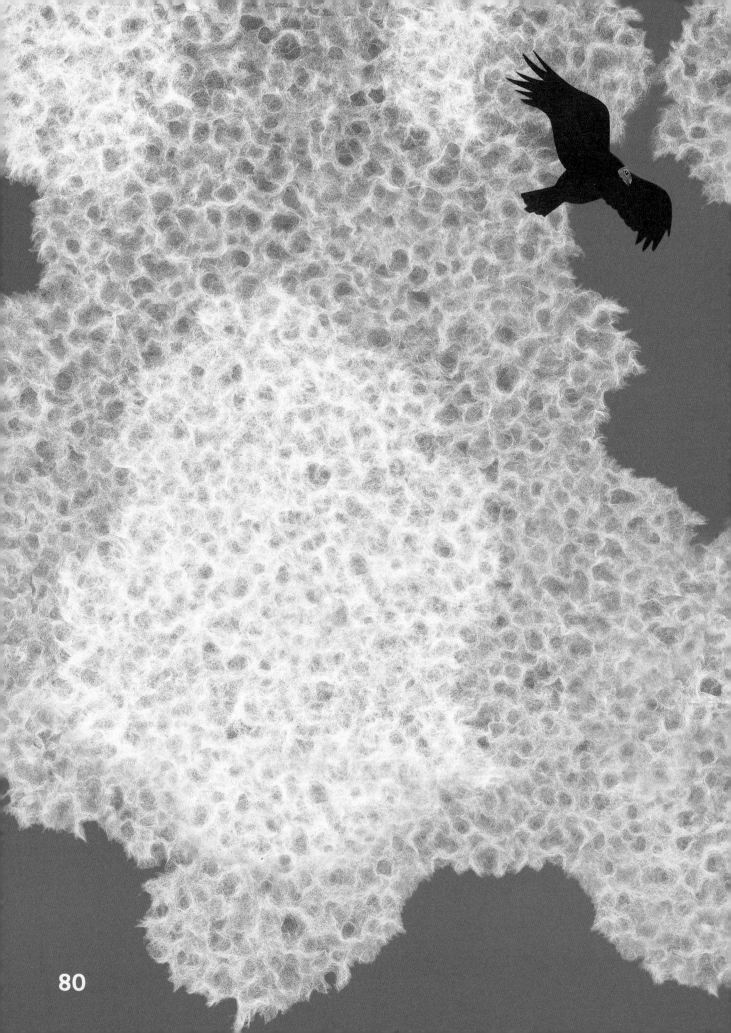

They hop, flap, soar
to look for **more**.
All afternoon.
But soon . . .

. . . the sun **starts** to sink.
Down, down.
The air starts to cool.
Down, down.
Wings glide, wings ride
through cooling air.

Going where?
Going down, down, down!

The vultures gather in vulture trees,
settle and sleep, like families.

Until . . .

. . . the morning sun rises.
Up, up.

It heats the air.
Up, up.

Wings stretch wide
to catch a ride
on warming air.
Going where?

Up, up!

Meet the Author

April Pulley Sayre loves science. She especially likes to come up with creative ways to tell stories about things in nature.

Meet the Illustrator

Steve Jenkins loves science, too. When he was growing up, he thought he would be a scientist, but he went to art school instead. Many of the books he illustrates are about animals.

Author's Purpose

April Pulley Sayre wanted to write about what a turkey vulture eats. Draw a picture of another bird eating. Write what the bird eats.

Respond to the Text

Retell

Use your own words to retell the main idea and important details in *Vulture View.*

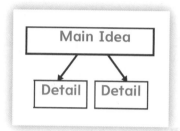

Write

How do vultures use their body parts to help them find food? Use these sentence starters:

The author says that vultures...
This helps them find food because...

Make Connections

COLLABORATE

Think of a wild animal you know. What does it eat and how does it get its food?

ESSENTIAL QUESTION

Compare Texts

Read about how a mouse survives winter.

When It's Snowing

by Aileen Fisher

Little Mouse, with narrow feet
that you keep so white and neat,
when it's snowing, freezing, blowing,
do you get enough to eat?

You're too little, Mouse, to stray
from your house on such a day.
Weren't you wise to gather scores
of munchy seeds to eat indoors!

Make Connections

? What does the little
mouse do to survive?

Essential Question

Illustration: Roberta Baird

91

Essential Question

What insects do you know? How are they alike and different?

Read about a fun pet who happens to be a fly.

Go Digital!

by Tedd Arnold

Chapter 1

A fly went flying.

He was looking for something to eat—

something tasty,

something slimy.

A boy went walking.

He was looking for
something to catch—
something smart,
something for
The Amazing Pet Show.

They met.

The boy **caught** the fly
in a jar.
"A pet!" he said.

The fly was mad.
He wanted to be free.
He stomped his foot
and said—

BUZZ!

The boy was surprised.
He said, "You **know** my name!
You are the smartest pet in
the world!"

Chapter 2

Buzz took the fly home.

"This is my pet," Buzz said
to Mom and Dad.

"He is smart. He can say
my name. **Listen!**"

Buzz opened the jar.
The fly **flew** out.

"Flies can't be pets!" said
Dad. "They are pests!"
He got the fly swatter.
The fly cried—

BUZZ!

And Buzz came to the rescue.
"You are right," said Dad.
"This fly _is_ smart!"

"He needs a name," said Mom.
Buzz thought for a minute.
"Fly Guy," said Buzz.
And Fly Guy said—

BUZZ!

It was time for lunch.
Buzz gave Fly Guy
something to eat.

Fly Guy was happy.

Chapter 3

Buzz took Fly Guy to
The Amazing Pet Show.

The judges **laughed**.
"Flies can't be pets," they said.
"Flies are pests!"

Buzz was sad.
He opened the jar.
"Shoo, Fly Guy," he said.
"Flies can't be pets."

But Fly Guy liked Buzz.
He had an idea.
He did some **fancy** flying.

The judges **were** amazed.
"The fly can do tricks,"
they said. "But flies can't
be pets."

Then Fly Guy said—

The judges were more amazed. "The fly knows the boy's name," they said. "But flies can't be pets."

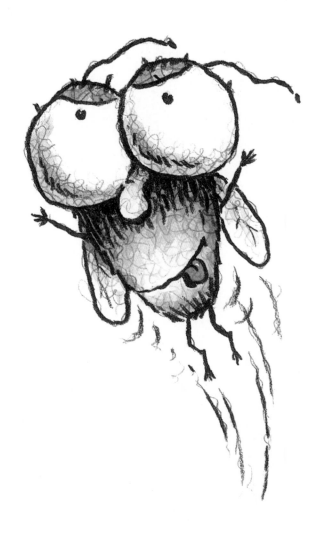

Fly Guy flew high, high, high
into the sky!

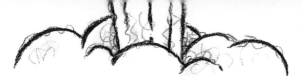

Then he dived down, down, down into the jar.

"The fly knows his jar!" the judges said. "This fly _is_ a pet!" So they let Fly Guy in the show.

He even won an award.

And so began a
beautiful friendship.

Meet Tedd Arnold

Tedd Arnold says, "My ideas come from different places at different times. A few years ago, it seemed like wherever I went with my family there was a pesky fly buzzing around us. Finally I decided to write a story about that little guy."

Author's Purpose

Tedd Arnold wanted to tell the story of an insect he knew about. Write about an insect you know. Draw a picture to go with your story.

Respond to the Text

Use your own words to retell *Hi! Fly Guy*. Your notes from your chart can help.

Character	Clue	Point of View

Write

Why do Buzz's parents and the judges change their minds about Fly Guy? Use these sentence starters:

At the beginning, they think...
Then Fly Guy...
At the end, they think...

Make Connections
COLLABORATE

How is Fly Guy like an insect you know? How is he different?
ESSENTIAL QUESTION

(bl) marcouliana/iStock/Getty Images; (tr) Anthony Bannister/Gallo Images/Corbis; (c) Ingram Publishing/SuperStock; (b, cr, tl) Burke/Triolo Productions/Brand X Pictures/Getty Images; (cl) Ale-ks/iStock/Getty Images

Meet the Insects

We can find insects all around the globe.
Insects can be lots of shapes, sizes, and
colors. There are more insects than any
other kind of animal.

How can you tell if a bug is an insect?
Read on to find out.

The Body of an Insect

All insects have six legs and three **body** parts. Insects have no bones. The outside of an insect's body is hard. It **protects** the insect's body. Most insects have antennae and wings.

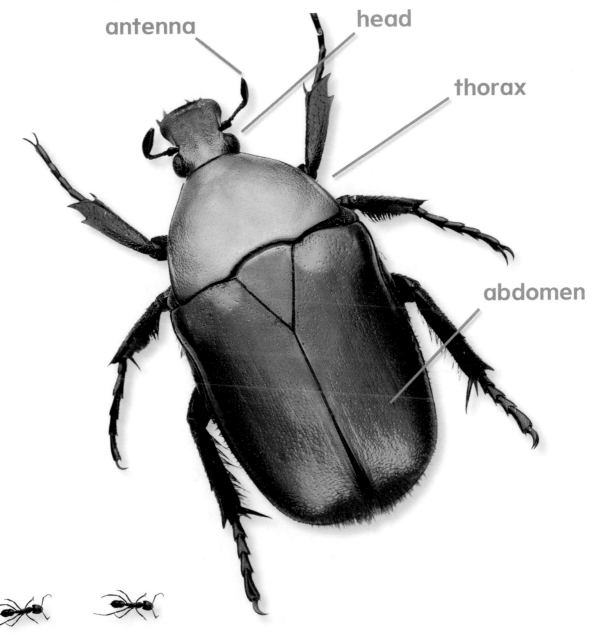

antenna

head

thorax

abdomen

Insect Senses

Insects use their **senses** to find food.
A fly smells with its antennae.
It tastes with its feet. That's
why flies like to land on food.

Insects do not see the same as we do.
Many insects have more than two eyes.
A grasshopper has five!

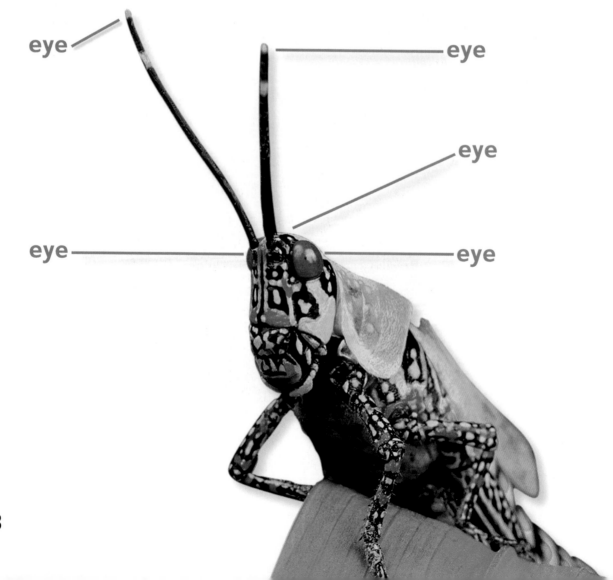

eye

eye

eye

eye

eye

Fun Insect Facts

Some ants can lift 20–100 times their own weight. This ant lifts a leaf.

A dragonfly can fly 22–30 miles an hour.

Termites build big mounds. They can be up to 30 feet high.

Insects are amazing!

Make Connections

What amazing thing could an ant do in a story? **Essential Question**

(tr) Peter Lilja/The Image Bank/Getty Images; (cr) NAOKI MUTAI/a collect/age fotostock; (b) Burke/Triolo Productions/Brand X Pictures/Getty Images; (br) Howard Birnstihl/age fotostock

Ronald Cohn/The Gorilla Foundation/koko.org

Essential Question

How do people work with animals?

Read about a gorilla who did amazing things.

Go Digital!

KOKO AND PENNY

What did a special teacher help Koko the gorilla do?

Koko was a gorilla. A **woman** named Penny Patterson wanted to see what Koko could do.

Koko was very young when Penny began teaching her.

Penny **found** baby Koko at a zoo in 1972. Koko was a year old. Koko jumped into Penny's arms and pulled her **near**. Penny liked Koko. She wanted to study her.

Penny wanted to teach Koko words. She showed her hand signs and **signals**. At first, Koko mostly asked for things she wanted. She **would** say words like "cookie" a lot!

This is how Koko said "sip."

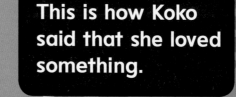

This is how Koko said that she loved something.

This is how Koko said "toothbrush."

But soon Koko could say more. She learned over 1,000 words! When she was happy, Koko would smile. When she was sad, she pointed to her eyes. This meant "cry." Koko was really **clever**!

Then Penny wanted to teach Koko how to do more things. She showed her how to use a pencil and paper. Koko worked **hard**. She even tried to **write** her name!

Koko liked to write notes. She was able to sign her own name.

Ronald Cohn/The Gorilla Foundation/koko.org

Koko was very gentle with her pets.

When Koko was 12, she would sign the word "cat" a lot. So Penny gave her a kitten. Koko was really kind to her kitty. She named him All Ball. She had many more pets and was always kind to all of them.

Koko had lots of projects. She was always busy. One of Koko's hobbies was painting. Koko painted many things. Koko liked to name her paintings. She named two paintings "Bird" and "Love."

Koko's favorite color was red.

Koko and Penny worked and played together for a long time! Koko and Penny were quite a team.

Respond to the Text

1. Use details from the selection to retell. SUMMARIZE

2. What benefits did Koko gain by learning sign language? WRITE

3. What can you learn from studying animals? TEXT TO WORLD

Compare Texts

Read about how you can help save bees.

Save Our Bees!

Beekeepers work with bees.

Bees need our help! Many bees are dying. Scientists think that bugs or diseases are hurting bees.

Bees are important to us. They help our crops grow. They make honey.

This bee has a bug on it. Bugs can make bees sick.

Bees like flowers.

You can make a difference! You can help bees by planting flowers. Bees eat nectar from flowers.

You can also build a bee block. Bees can build nests in a bee block. But *bee* careful! Bees can sting.

Together we can help save our bees!

This is a bee block. You can make it out of wood.

Make Connections

How is helping bees similar to what Penny did to help Koko? How is it different? **Essential Question**

Genre Fantasy

Essential Question

How can we classify and categorize things?

Read about what happens when Toad loses his button.

Go Digital!

A Lost Button

from **Frog and Toad Are Friends**

by Arnold Lobel

Toad and Frog

went for a long walk.

They walked across

a **large** meadow.

They walked in the woods.

They walked along the river.

At last they went back home

to Toad's house.

"Oh, drat," said Toad.

"Not **only** do my feet hurt,

but I have lost

one of the buttons on my jacket."

"Don't worry," said Frog.

"We will go back

to all the places where we walked.

We will soon find your button."

They walked back to the large meadow.

They began to look for the button

in the tall grass.

"Here is your button!" cried Frog.

"That is not my button," said Toad.

"That button is black.

My button was white."

Toad **put** the black button

in his pocket.

A sparrow flew down.

"Excuse me," said the sparrow.

"Did you lose a button? I found one."

"That is not my button," said Toad.

"That button has two holes.

My button had **four** holes."

Toad put the button with two holes

in his pocket.

They went back to the woods
and looked on the dark paths.
"Here is your button," said Frog.
"That is not my button," cried Toad.
"That button is small.
My button was big."
Toad put the small button
in his pocket.

A raccoon came out from behind a tree.

"I heard that you were looking

for a button," he said.

"Here is one that I just found."

"That is not my button!" wailed Toad.

"That button is square.

My button was **round**."

Toad put the square button

in his pocket.

Frog and Toad went back to the river.

They looked for the button

in the mud.

"Here is your button," said Frog.

"That is not my button!" shouted Toad.

"That button is thin.

My button was thick."

Toad put the thin button
in his pocket. He was very angry.
He jumped up and down
and screamed,
"The **whole** world
is covered with buttons,
and not one of them is mine!"

Toad ran home and slammed the door.

There, on the floor,

he saw his white, four-holed,

big, round, thick button.

"Oh," said Toad.

"It was here all the time.

What a lot of **trouble**

I have made for Frog."

Toad took all of the buttons

out of his pocket.

He took his sewing box

down from the shelf.

Toad sewed the buttons

all over his jacket.

The next day Toad gave

his jacket to Frog.

Frog thought that it was beautiful.

He put it on and jumped for joy.

None of the buttons fell off.

Toad had sewed them on very well.

Meet Arnold Lobel

Arnold Lobel was often sick and missed many days of school when he was young. When he went back to school, he made friends by telling stories and drawing pictures.

Many years later, Lobel's children liked to catch frogs and toads. Lobel loved the animals and wrote about them in his Frog and Toad stories.

Author's Purpose

Arnold Lobel wanted to write about good friends. Write about your friend. Tell how you help each other.

Respond to the Text

Retell

Use your own words to retell "A Lost Button" from *Frog and Toad Are Friends.*

Character	Clue	Point of View

Write

Do you think that Frog or Toad was the better friend in "A Lost Button"? Why? Use these sentence frames:

I think the better friend was...
He was a better friend because...

Make Connections

COLLABORATE

What are all the ways Toad describes his button?
ESSENTIAL QUESTION

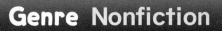

Compare Texts

Read about the different ways to sort objects and animals.

Sort It Out

Some things are **alike**. Some are **different**. We can **sort** things by looking at what is the same about them. We can sort them by their size, shape, and color.

Find the buttons in this picture. Let's sort them!

How many round buttons can you see?
How many square buttons can you see?
What other shapes do you see?
Add up the number of red buttons.
Are there more red or yellow buttons?
Can you find buttons with four holes?
How else could you sort these buttons?

We can sort animals, too.
We can sort animals by features.
Which animals have four legs?
Which animals have two legs?
Which have none?
Which animals have patterns?
Which animals have yellow?
Which are bigger than you are?

We can classify animals by type.
Which are birds?
Which are reptiles?
Which are mammals?
What other types of
animals can you see?

159

Sorting is a lot of fun! Let's sort things in this scene. Think about what they have in common.

Which of these things have wheels?
Which eat food?
Which can fly?
Which have stripes?
Which have windows?
Which would you play with?

Illustration: Holli Conger

There are lots of ways to sort the things in this scene. Think of as many ways as you can.

Make Connections

How can we sort objects?
How can we sort animals?

Essential Question

161

Essential Question

What can you see in the sky?

Read about a kitten who thinks the moon is a bowl of milk.

Go Digital!

It was Kitten's first full moon.

When she saw it, she thought,

There's a little bowl of milk in the sky.

And she wanted it.

So she closed her eyes
and **stretched** her neck
and opened her mouth and licked.

But Kitten only ended up
with a bug on her tongue.
Poor Kitten!

Still, there was the little bowl

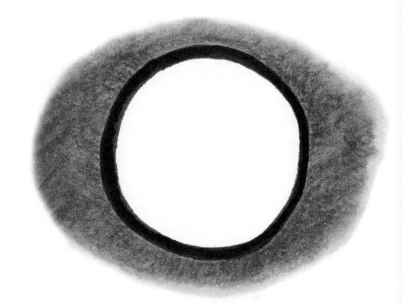

of milk, just waiting.

So she pulled herself together

and wiggled her bottom

and sprang from the top step of the porch.

But Kitten only tumbled—
bumping her nose and banging her ear
and pinching her tail.
Poor Kitten!

Still, there was the little bowl

of milk, just waiting.

So she chased it—
down the sidewalk,
   through the garden,
      past the field,
         and by the pond.
But Kitten never seemed to get closer.
Poor Kitten!

Still, there was the little bowl

of milk, just waiting.

So she ran
to the tallest tree
she could find,
and she **climbed**
and climbed
and climbed
to the very top.

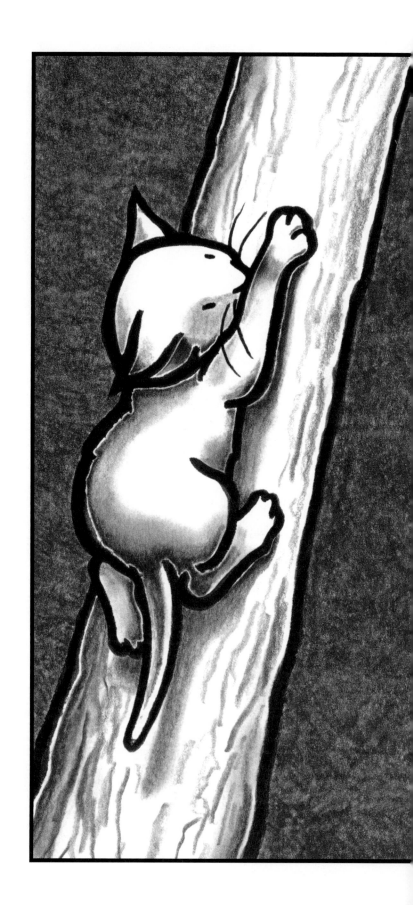

But Kitten
still couldn't reach
the bowl of milk,
and now she was
scared.
Poor Kitten!
What could she do?

Then, in the pond, Kitten saw
another bowl of milk.
And it was bigger.
What a night!

So she raced down the tree

and raced through the grass

and raced to the edge of the pond.

She leaped with all her might—

Poor Kitten!

She was wet and sad and tired and hungry.

So she went

back home—

187

and there was

a great big

bowl of milk

    on the porch,

just waiting for her.

Lucky Kitten!

Meet Kevin Henkes

Kevin Henkes got the idea for *Kitten's First Full Moon* from a story he had begun to write many years before. Although he never finished this story, there was a line that read, "The cat thought the moon was a bowl of milk." He couldn't get this line out of his head, and slowly over the years the story of *Kitten's First Full Moon* formed.

Author's Purpose

Kevin Henkes got his story idea from a line he liked. Can you think of a line from a rhyme or story that you like? Draw and write about it.

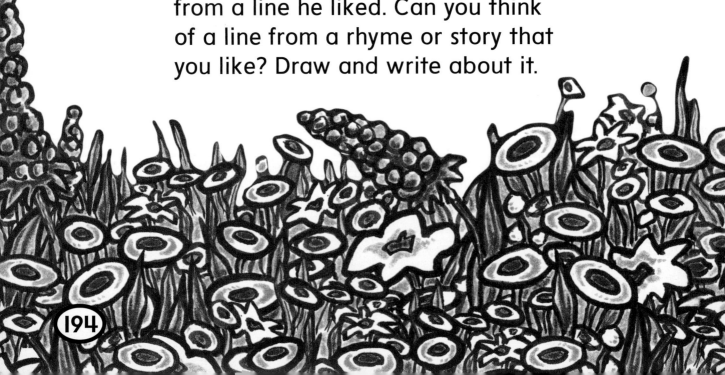

Respond to the Text

Use your own words to retell *Kitten's First Full Moon.* The information on your Cause and Effect chart can help.

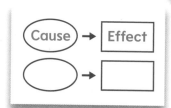

Write

Why couldn't Kitten drink the milk in the sky? How do you know? Use these sentence frames:

Kitten couldn't drink the milk because...
Kitten thought...

Make Connections

COLLABORATE

How is the moon like a bowl of milk? What else could the moon look like?
ESSENTIAL QUESTION

THE MOON

The Night Sky

Think of what you see in the night sky. You see stars and the Moon.

The Moon is the neighbor closest to **Earth** in space. But it is very far away. The Moon is about 239,000 miles from Earth!

The Moon looks much smaller than it really is because it is so far away.

On some nights the Moon looks bright and round. But it does not make its own light. Light from the sun shines on the Moon. The light bounces back to Earth. We only see the lighted part of the Moon that faces Earth.

The Moon looks different every day of the month.

Why doesn't the Moon look round every night?

The Moon moves in a circle around the Earth.

As it circles, part of the Moon faces the sun.

We see the part of the Moon that is lighted.
That's why the Moon seems to change shape.

We can see the Moon better with a telescope.

Some people once thought that the Moon was made of cheese. Others saw the face of a man in the Moon.

Then **telescopes** helped us see the Moon better. The telescopes showed hills and flat places. They showed craters, or big holes, too.

Then, in 1961, astronauts went into space.
In 1969, other astronauts walked on the Moon!
They got a real close-up look.

Nothing grows on the Moon. It is very rocky.
Astronauts brought back Moon rocks
for us to see.

Maybe one day you will go
to the Moon, too!

Astronauts went into
space and landed on
the Moon.

Make Connections

What kind of Moon did Kitten
in *Kitten's First Full Moon* see?
Would she try to catch the Moon
every night? **Essential Question**

Essential Question

What inventions do you know about?

Read about inventor Thomas Edison.

Go Digital!

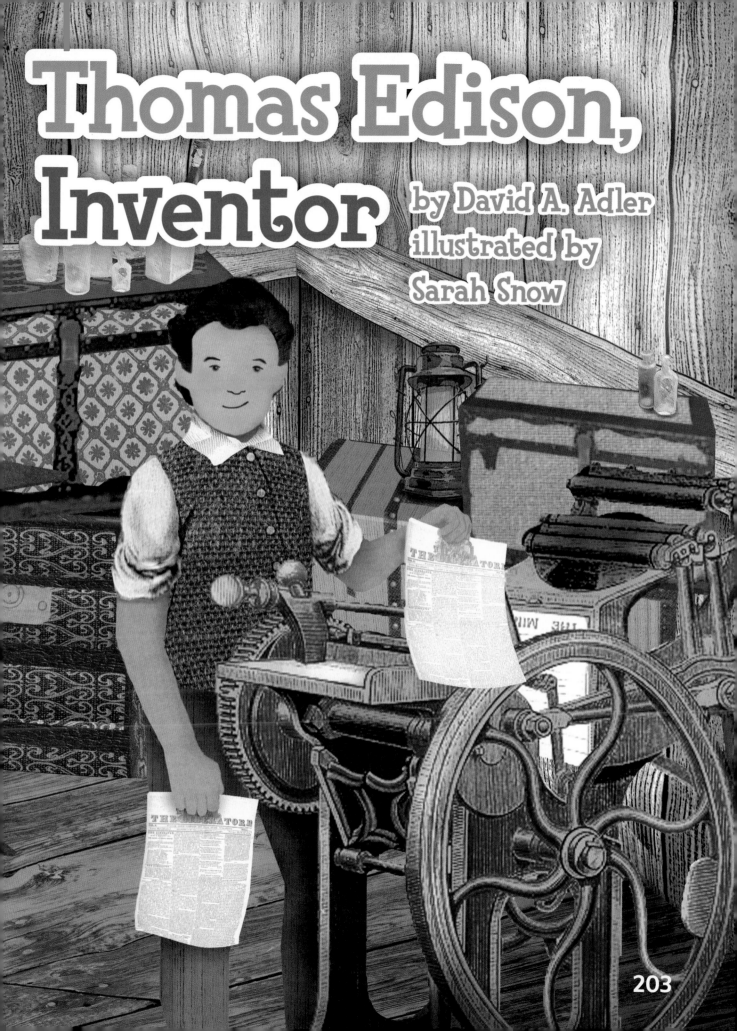

Thomas Edison, Inventor

by David A. Adler

illustrated by

Sarah Snow

Chapter 1

Young Tom Edison asked lots of questions. When someone told him, "I don't know," Tom had one more question. He asked, "Why don't you know?" He did lots of experiments to find out.

Tom watched a goose sit on some eggs. He saw the eggs hatch. He wanted to know what would happen if he sat on eggs.

So, Tom made a nest. Then, he put goose and chicken eggs in the nest. Next, he sat on the eggs and found out. Splat!

Young Tom also knew that birds ate worms and birds could fly. What if people ate worms? Tom **guessed** that they would fly, too.

So, he gave a girl a cup of chopped worms and water. The girl drank it and got sick. And she didn't fly.

Tom Edison, the boy who asked all those
questions and did those **unusual** experiments,
became the man whose inventions changed
the world.

Tom Edison was born in 1847 in Milan, Ohio. He was the seventh and youngest child of Sam and Nancy Edison.

Sam had a lumber mill. Nancy had been a teacher. When Tom had trouble in school, his mother became his teacher at home.

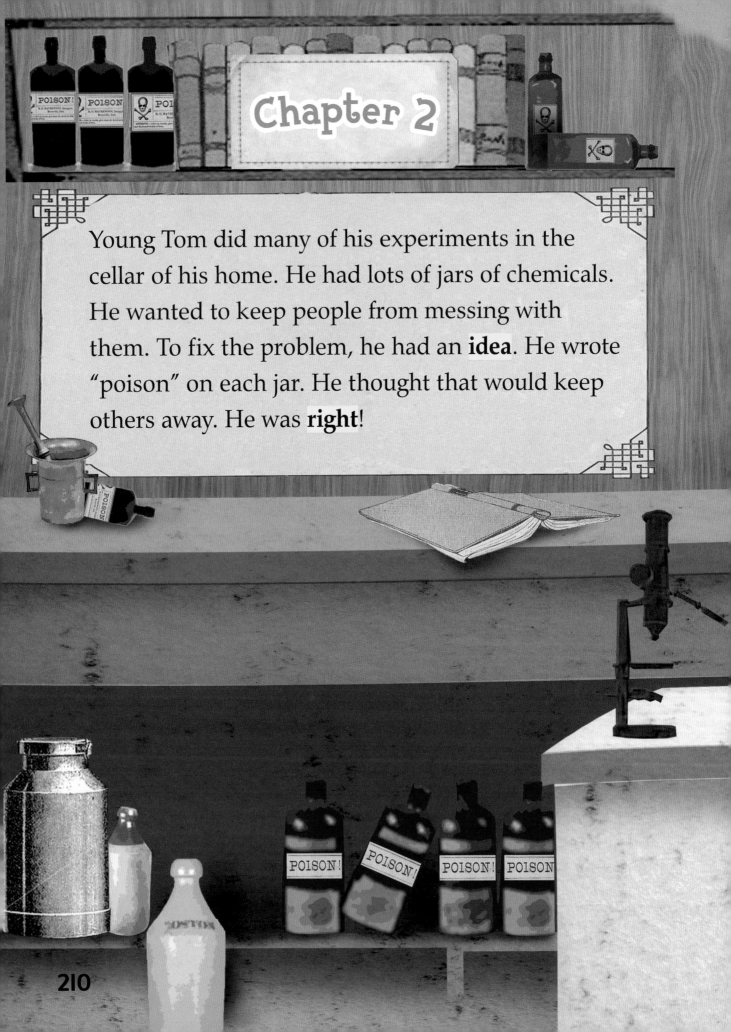

Chapter 2

Young Tom did many of his experiments in the cellar of his home. He had lots of jars of chemicals. He wanted to keep people from messing with them. To fix the problem, he had an **idea**. He wrote "poison" on each jar. He thought that would keep others away. He was **right**!

There were often smoke, strange smells, and loud noises in the Edison home. It all came from the cellar and from young Tom's experiments.

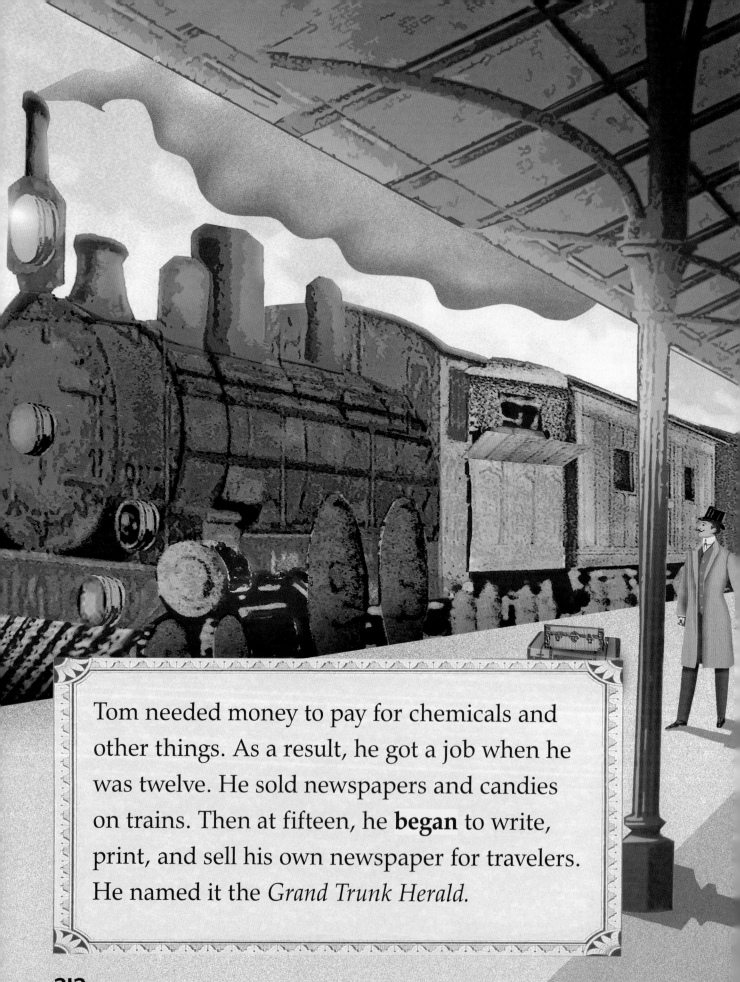

Tom needed money to pay for chemicals and other things. As a result, he got a job when he was twelve. He sold newspapers and candies on trains. Then at fifteen, he **began** to write, print, and sell his own newspaper for travelers. He named it the *Grand Trunk Herald*.

Tom wrote news of people he met on the train. He also wrote how he felt about work. "The more to do," he wrote in his newspaper, "the more done." Tom liked to keep busy. Tom kept very busy on the train. He even set up his own lab in the baggage car.

As Tom got older, he kept doing great things. There were no telephones at the time. Instead, messages were sent through telegraph wires. They were sent in a code of dots and dashes.

Tom **learned** the code. He got a job sending and reading telegraph messages. He found new ways to use the telegraph. Those were some of his first inventions.

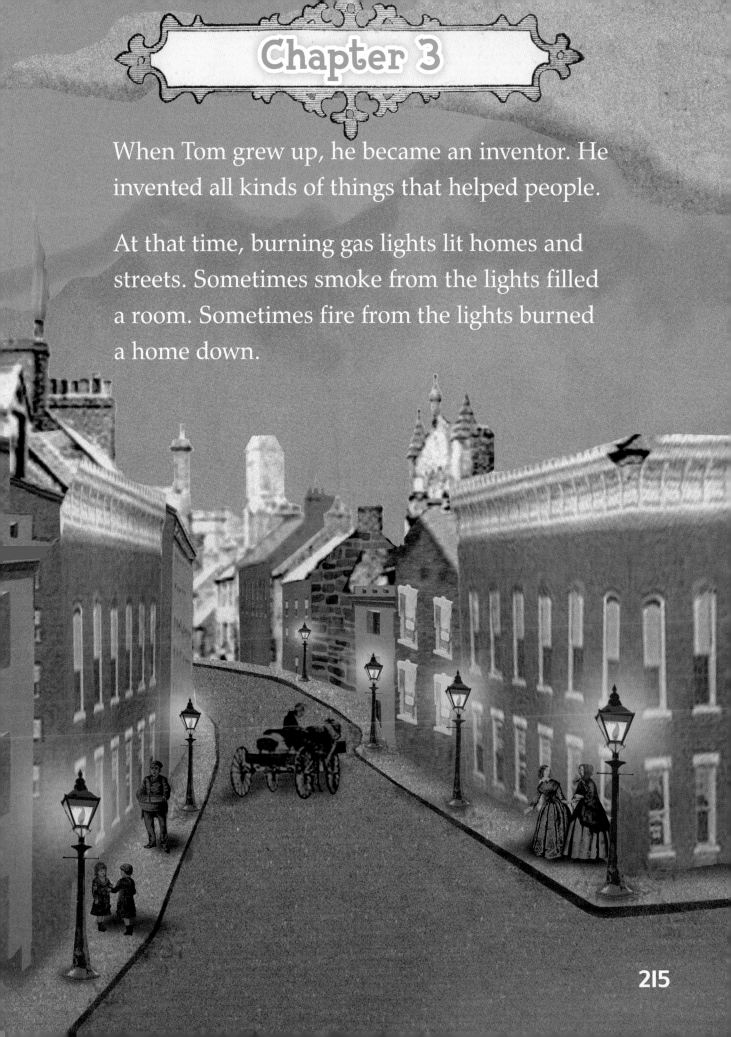

Chapter 3

When Tom grew up, he became an inventor. He invented all kinds of things that helped people.

At that time, burning gas lights lit homes and streets. Sometimes smoke from the lights filled a room. Sometimes fire from the lights burned a home down.

Tom was **sure** he could make a **better** light. So, he did experiments with electric light. He had lots of ideas. His notes filled hundreds of notebooks.

After more than a year of work, Tom did it. He made a light that was safe to use.

"The electric light is the light of the future," Tom said. "And it will be my light."

216

Edison's lights were big news. People came
from all over to see them. Once they saw
the Edison lights, they wanted them in their
homes. Tom's lights brightened the world.

Tom Edison spent his whole life making
great things. The things he made helped
people everywhere.

Thomas Edison Photo Album

Thomas Alva Edison at age 15.

Edison invented the first machine that could record sounds and play them back. Without this, we might have no music players or movies and TV with sound today!

Edison made this early music player using his own sound machine.

Thomas Edison in his lab in Menlo Park, New Jersey.

Edison's lightbulb design looks similar to ones we use today.

Edison invented the first machine for viewing films. Without this machine, there would be no movies!

Meet the Author

David A. Adler says, "I love to write. With Tom Edison's invention, the light bulb, I can write even after the sun goes down."

David Adler has written all kinds of fiction and nonfiction for children. He especially likes writing biographies of people who acted in ways that children can learn from.

Author's Purpose

David A. Adler wanted to tell how curious Tom Edison was even when he was a boy. Think of something you are curious about. Write your question and how you could find the answer.

Respond to the Text

Retell

Use your own words to retell *Thomas Edison, Inventor.* Information from your chart can help.

Problem
↓
Steps to Solution
↓
Solution

Write

What can you tell about what made Thomas Edison a good inventor? Use these sentence starters:

> As a boy, Thomas Edison...
> When he got older, he...

Make Connections

COLLABORATE

How do electric lights make your life better?
ESSENTIAL QUESTION

Compare Texts

Read about two inventions
you know well.

Windshield Wipers

by Rebecca Kai Dotlich

Squish, squish,
squeegy-squish
tossing rain
side   to   side;
squish, squish,
squeegy-squish,
flap, flap,
puddle glide.
Slosh, slosh,
sloshing wash,
plish, plish,
tidal toss.
Squeegy-squish,
squish, squish, sway…

a perfect windshield
wiper day.

Scissors

by Rebecca Kai Dotlich

X slides open,
squeezes shut—
snip, snip, snip,
carve,
cut.

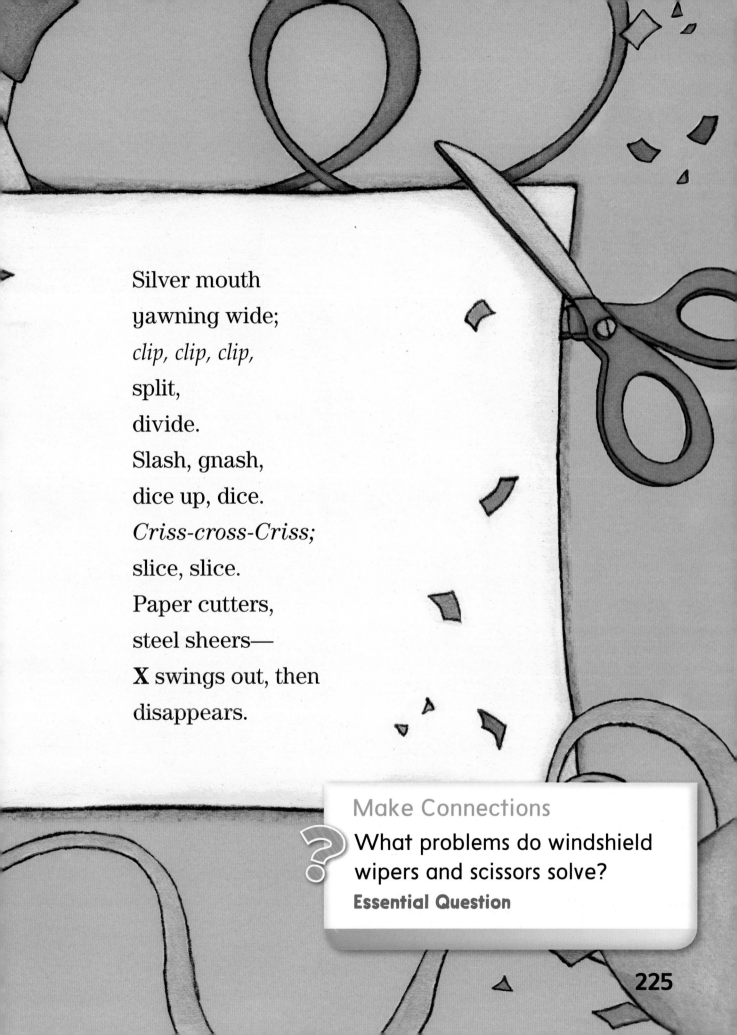

Silver mouth
yawning wide;
clip, clip, clip,
split,
divide.
Slash, gnash,
dice up, dice.
Criss-cross-Criss;
slice, slice.
Paper cutters,
steel sheers—
X swings out, then
disappears.

Make Connections

? What problems do windshield
wipers and scissors solve?
Essential Question

Genre Realistic Fiction

Essential Question

What sounds can you hear? How are they made?

Read about a boy who wants to whistle.

Go Digital!

Whistle for Willie

by Ezra Jack Keats

Oh, how Peter wished he could whistle!

He saw a boy playing with his dog. Whenever the boy whistled, the dog ran straight to him.

Peter tried and tried to whistle, but he couldn't.
So **instead** he began to turn himself around—
around and around he whirled ...
faster and faster....

When he stopped
everything turned
down ...
and up ...

and up ...
and down ...
and around
and around.

Peter saw his dog, Willie, coming.
Quick as a wink, he hid in an empty
carton lying on the sidewalk.

"Wouldn't it be funny if I whistled?" Peter **thought**.
"Willie would stop and look all around to see
who it was."

Peter tried again to whistle—but still he couldn't.
So Willie just walked on.

Peter got out of the carton
and started home.
On the way he took some
colored chalks out of his pocket
and drew a long, long line
right up to his door.

He stood there and tried to whistle again.
He blew till his cheeks were tired.
But **nothing** happened.

He went into his house and put on his father's old hat to make himself feel more grown up. He looked into the mirror to practice whistling.
Still no whistle!

When his mother saw what he was doing,
Peter pretended that he was his father.

He said, "I've come home **early** today,
dear. Is Peter here?"

His mother answered, "Why no, he's
outside with Willie."

"Well, I'll go out and look for them,"
said Peter.

First he walked along a crack in the
sidewalk. Then he tried to run away
from his shadow.

He jumped off his shadow,
but when he landed they were
together again.

He came to the corner where the carton was, and who should he see but Willie!

Peter **scrambled** under the carton.
He blew and blew and blew.
Suddenly—out came a real whistle!

Willie stopped and looked around to see
who it was.

"It's me," Peter shouted, and stood up.
Willie raced straight to him.

Peter ran home to show his father and mother
what he could do. They loved Peter's whistling.
So did Willie.

Peter's mother asked him and Willie to go
on an errand to the grocery store.

He whistled all the way there,
and he whistled all the way home.

Meet Ezra Jack Keats

Ezra Jack Keats sold his first painting when he was eight years old! When he grew up, he created many books for children. He used cut-out paper and a special type of paste to make the bright pictures. He won many awards for his work, but he was most pleased by letters from children who had read his books.

Author's Purpose

Ezra Jack Keats wanted to write about a boy who wished he could whistle. Write about something you wish you could do. Tell why you want to do it.

Ezra Jack Keats

Respond to the Text

Retell

Use your own words to retell *Whistle for Willie.*

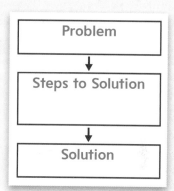

Problem
↓
Steps to Solution
↓
Solution

Write

Write a new story about a time Peter learned to play a musical instrument or to sing a special song. Use these sentence starters:

> Peter wanted to...
> Peter tried...

Make Connections

COLLABORATE

What other sounds could Peter use to get Willie's attention?
ESSENTIAL QUESTION

Compare Texts

Learn how to make instruments.

Shake! Strike! Strum!

Shake, strike, strum! **Instruments** can be a lot of fun. Instruments make different kinds of sounds. Strike a drum. Rum-pum-pum. Strum a guitar. Plink, pling. Blow on a horn. Toot, toot. Shake it up!

Some sounds are nice to hear. Others are not. But all sounds have two things in common: pitch and volume.

Pitch is how high or low a sound is. When you whistle for a dog, you make a high-pitched sound.

Volume is how loud or soft a sound is. When you whisper in class, you make a low-volume sound.

You can make fun sounds too. Make these instruments and start a band!

How to Make a Guitar

What You Need

- tissue box
- rubber bands
- tape
- ruler

What to Do

1. Stretch four to six rubber bands around the box.

2. Tape a ruler to the back. This is the guitar's neck.

3. Decorate the guitar.

4. Strum or pluck the rubber bands.

How to Make a Shaker

What You Need

- plastic bottle
- dried beans
- stickers

What to Do

1. Put beans into the bottle.
2. Put fun stickers on it.
3. Shake it and have fun.

Now you can shake, strike, strum, and have some fun!

Make Connections

? How are sounds different? What sounds can you make? **Essential Question**

Essential Question

How do things get built?

Read about different kinds of bridges.

Go Digital!

Building Bridges

What kinds of bridges are there? How are they built?

1,125 feet

People **build** bridges to get from one point to another. Bridges go across water or land. They can be miles long or only a few feet.

Let's look at some of the world's most interesting bridges!

This bridge in France goes across a wide valley. It is the highest car bridge in the world.

The Sunshine Skyway Bridge in Florida stretches for four miles. This is a cable-stayed bridge. Sturdy wires help this bridge stay up. The wires are joined at tall towers so they don't **fall**.

This bridge is made of steel and concrete.

This bridge is more than 2,000 years old.

An arch bridge is like an upside-down U. This bridge has two big arches for boats to go through. The arches are the same size which helps **balance** the bridge. This bridge in Italy is made of brick, so it is really sturdy.

263

This bridge is
made of steel.

The Firth of Forth Bridge in Scotland is
a truss bridge. It is built **above** a river.
Do you see the triangles? The roadway
needs to be supported. The triangle tubes
support it. The triangles join each **section**
of the bridge.

Cars pay a toll, or **money**, to cross the Golden Gate Bridge in California. This suspension bridge has cables. The cables are supported by towers. Why is the bridge painted a bright color? The builders **knew** it must stand out in the fog. So they avoided colors like gray and painted it joyful orange.

The Golden Gate Bridge is a famous symbol of the United States.

Ed Pritchard/Stone/Getty Images

265

The bridge is flat so that people can cross.

Some bridges are one-of-a-kind. Rolling Bridge is in London, England. What happens when a boat comes **toward** the bridge? The bridge rises up and curls into a circle. Then the boat can pass.

There are many kinds of bridges. What kind of bridge can you think up?

Steve Speller/Alamy

When a boat passes the bridge begins to move.

Then the bridge becomes a circle.

Respond to the Text

1. Use details from the selection to retell. SUMMARIZE

2. Which bridge do you think is the most interesting? Why? WRITE

3. What is the same about how all bridges are built?

TEXT TO WORLD

Compare Texts

Read about a tiny building.

Small JOY

Tiny houses can go where their owners go!

Many people live in tiny houses. Tiny houses look small, but they feel big inside. This tiny house has one bedroom and one bathroom.

Dee Williams

Dee climbs a ladder to get to her bedroom.

This tiny kitchen has everything Dee needs.

Tiny houses do not take a long time to build. Tiny houses do not cost a lot. And tiny houses do not take up a lot of energy or materials. They are good for the earth!

Make Connections

 What would you have in your tiny house? **Essential Question**

CLICK CLACK MOO: COWS THAT TYPE by Doreen Cronin, illustrated by Betsy Lewin. Text copyright © 2000 by Doreen Cronin. Illustrations copyright © 2000 by Betsy Lewin. Reprinted by arrangement with Atheneum Books For Young Readers, an Imprint of Simon & Schuster Children's Publishing Division. All rights reserved.

Essential Question

How can we work together to make our lives better?

Read about how some smart cows and hens get what they want.

Go Digital!

Click, Clack, Moo
Cows That Type

by Doreen Cronin

illustrated by Betsy Lewin

Farmer Brown has a problem.
His cows like to type.
All day long he hears

Click, clack, **moo.**
Click, clack, **moo.**
Clickety, clack, **moo.**

At first, he couldn't believe his ears.
Cows that type.
Impossible!

Click, clack, **moo.**
Click, clack, **moo.**
Clickety, clack, **moo.**

273

Then, he couldn't believe his **eyes**.

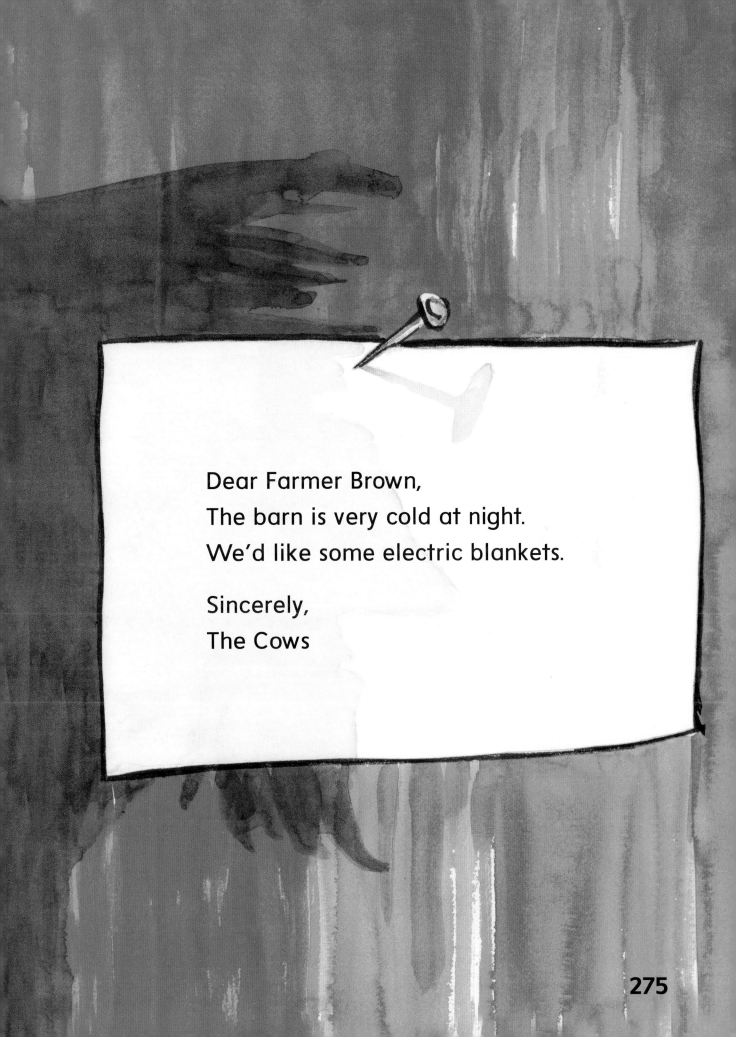

Dear Farmer Brown,
The barn is very cold at night.
We'd like some electric blankets.

Sincerely,
The Cows

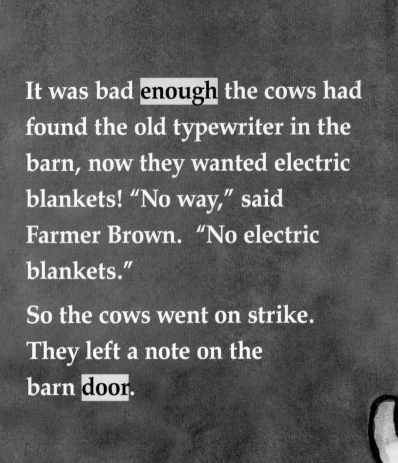

It was bad **enough** the cows had found the old typewriter in the barn, now they wanted electric blankets! "No way," said Farmer Brown. "No electric blankets."

So the cows went on strike. They left a note on the barn **door**.

"No milk today!" cried Farmer Brown. In the background, he heard the cows busy at work:

Click, clack, **moo.**
Click, clack, **moo.**
Clickety, clack, **moo.**

**The next day, he got
another note:**

Dear Farmer Brown,
The hens are cold too.
They'd like electric
blankets.

Sincerely,
The Cows

The cows were growing impatient with the farmer. They left a new note on the barn door.

"No eggs!" cried Farmer Brown.
In the background he heard them.

Click, clack, **moo.**
Click, clack, **moo.**
Clickety, clack, **moo.**

"Cows that type. Hens on strike! Whoever heard of such a thing? How can I run a farm with no milk and no eggs!" Farmer Brown was furious.

Farmer Brown got out his own typewriter.

Dear Cows and Hens:
There will be no electric blankets.
You are cows and hens.
I **demand** milk and eggs.

Sincerely,
Farmer Brown

Duck was a neutral party, so he brought the ultimatum to the cows.

The cows held an emergency meeting. All the animals gathered around the barn to snoop, but none of them could understand Moo.

All night long, Farmer Brown waited for an answer.

Duck knocked on the door early
the next morning. He handed
Farmer Brown a note:

Dear Farmer Brown,
We will exchange our typewriter
for electric blankets.
Leave them outside the barn door
and we will send Duck over with
the typewriter.

Sincerely,
The Cows

289

Farmer Brown decided this was
a good deal.

He left the blankets next to the barn
door and waited for Duck to come with
the typewriter.

The next morning he got a note:

Dear Farmer Brown,
The pond is quite boring.
We'd like a diving board.

Sincerely,
The Ducks

Click, clack, **quack.**
Click, clack, **quack.**
Clickety, clack, **quack.**

Meet the Author and Illustrator

Doreen

Betsy

Author Doreen Cronin and illustrator Betsy Lewin met for the first time after *Click, Clack, Moo: Cows That Type* was published.

Betsy says that she and Doreen have become good friends and enjoy working together. "Each of us is eager for the other's comments and advice."

Author's Purpose

Doreen Cronin and Betsy Lewin tell a story about how animals work together to get something they need. Write an idea for a story about kids who work together to get something they need.

Respond to the Text

Retell

Use your own words to retell *Click, Clack, Moo: Cows That Type.*

Clue
↓
Clue
↓
Clue
↓
Theme

Write

Imagine the farmer wouldn't give the ducks a diving board. Write a letter that he might receive from the animals after he says no. Use these sentence starters:

> Dear Farmer Brown, ...
> If we don't get a diving board...

Make Connections

COLLABORATE

What kind of deal might the ducks make with Farmer Brown?
ESSENTIAL QUESTION

Compare Texts

Read about what you can do to help make people's lives better.

These volunteers help at a food drive.

Be a Volunteer!

Do you want to help people improve their lives? You can become a volunteer!

People work at jobs to make money. They use the money to pay for things they need and want.

But did you know that sometimes people work for free? These people are called volunteers.

Why do people volunteer? That's easy. Volunteering is an important way to help others!

Volunteers can help people and animals. They can help our planet. There are many different ways to volunteer.

Volunteers can visit a nursing home.

These volunteers help in a garden.

People of all ages can be volunteers.

Let's read about how volunteers can clean up a lake!

When spring comes, a lake needs to be ready so that everyone can enjoy it in the summer. There are different jobs volunteers can do.

Volunteers can plants flowers and bushes. They can clear rocks and sticks from paths to make them safe for walking. Volunteers can also collect plastic bottles and cans to **recycle**.

Trash can end up on the edge of a lake. Volunteers can help remove items that don't belong in the water. They use special **equipment** to pick up the items. A clean lake is better for people and animals!

Volunteers wear special gloves to protect their hands.

Many families like to have picnics at the lake. Volunteers like you can pick up trash and plant flowers in picnic areas.

Now the lake is ready for picnic fun!

Please Keep Picnic Area Clean!

You can create a poster like this one to keep the picnic area or lake clean.

Together, volunteers can make a difference!

When volunteers work with each other, they can do big jobs.

You can do your part, too! Look for ways to volunteer in your community.

Everyone should be a volunteer!

 Make Connections

How are the volunteers in "Be a Volunteer!" like the cows in *Click, Clack, Moo: Cows That Type*? **Essential Question**

Genre Nonfiction

? **Essential Question**
Who helps you?
Read about a girl who is a lot like you!

Go Digital!

Meet Rosina

by George Ancona

(bl) The McGraw-Hill Companies, Inc; (br) Stockbyte/PunchStock

303

Hi! I'm

 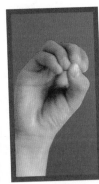    

R o s i n a

I am deaf, so I talk with my hands.

I go to a special school for deaf children. All of our teachers teach with American Sign Language. We call this signing.

We study math, writing, reading, and art. It's the same as in other schools.

My **brother** Emilio also goes to my school. We play basketball during recess.

307

My **mother** and aunt are deaf, too. They both work at my school. Mom is a teacher's helper.

My Aunt Carla shows us **pictures** of students who used to go to the school. My mom was one of them. My aunt **often** tells stories about when my parents were young.

Sometimes we go to the school library.
Our librarian, Hedy, signs stories from
the books in the library.

Hedy is good at telling stories. She makes us feel as if we're in the story. The story can make us feel sad, scared, worried, or happy.

311

I **love** going to art class. I like to paint. Here I am painting a picture of myself!

Our class made up a story. It is about a deaf **father** who woke up one day with four arms. We wrote it and did all the drawings. Then we made it into a book called *Too Many Hands.*

I like sports. We are playing rugby. The way we play is to tag the person carrying the ball. Then he or she throws it to another player on the team. By running fast we can get away and cross the goal line.

Our team played other schools. We beat all of the other teams and **accepted** a big trophy.

We were so happy! We splashed our coach in water. Some of us got wet, too. We are all **friends** so no one got mad.

After school I shower and change clothes for dinner. Mom likes to fix my hair. She puts it up in a bun like her mother did.

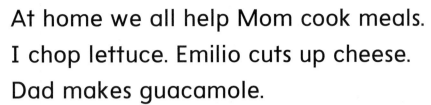
At home we all help Mom cook meals.
I chop lettuce. Emilio cuts up cheese.
Dad makes guacamole.

After dinner, Dad and I play a game of chess. Emilio roots for me.

Mom, Dad, Emilio, and me. That's my family—but there are many more, too.

We are a big family. I have lots of aunts, cousins, grandpas, and grandmas. Most of my mom's family is deaf. My whole family uses sign language to talk to each other.

This is how we sign "goodbye."

George Ancona wrote the words and took the photographs for this piece. He learned how to take photographs from his father when he was growing up. His father developed pictures in their bathroom!

Today, George likes to photograph people in their everyday lives. Before George wrote this book, he already knew some sign language. In this picture, he is signing, "I love you!"

Author's Purpose

George Ancona shows how Rosina spends a day. Write a journal entry about what you did yesterday.

George Ancona

Respond to the Text

Retell

Use your own words to retell *Meet Rosina.*

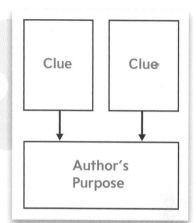

Clue   Clue

Author's Purpose

Write

Rosina has a special community that works together. How do the people in your community work together to help you? Use these sentence starters:

I get help from...
They help me by...

Make Connections

COLLABORATE

How does Rosina's family help her? Who else helps her? ESSENTIAL QUESTION

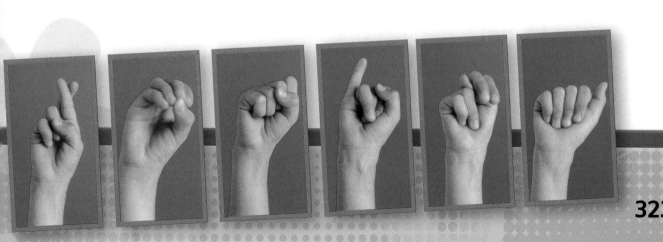

Compare Texts

Read about a grandmother who helps in her own special way.

Abuelita's Lap

by Pat Mora

I know a place where I can sit
and tell about my day,
tell every color that I saw
from green to cactus gray.

I know a place where I can sit
and hear a favorite beat,
her heart and *cuentos* from the past,
the rhythms honey-sweet.

I know a place where I can sit
and listen to a star,
listen to its silent song
gliding from afar.

I know a place where I can sit
and hear the wind go by,
hearing it spinning round my house,
my whirling lullaby.

Make Connections

How does the boy feel about his grandmother? **Essential Question**

Essential Question

How can weather affect us?

Read about why a school has to be rebuilt every year.

Go Digital!

Rain School

by James Rumford

In the **country** of Chad, it is the first day of school.
The dry dirt road is filling up with **children**.

Big brothers and big sisters are leading the way.

"Will they give us a notebook?" Thomas asks.

"Will they give us a pencil?"

"Will I learn to read like you?"

"Stop asking so many **questions** and keep up," say the big brothers and big sisters.

Thomas arrives at the schoolyard,
but there are no classrooms.

There are no desks.

It doesn't matter.

There is a teacher.

"We will build our school,"
she says. "This is the first lesson."

Thomas learns to make mud bricks
and dry them in the sun.

He learns to build mud walls and mud desks.

He **gathers** grass and saplings with the other children, and they make a roof.

Inside it is cool. It smells of the earth. It smells of the fields ready for planting.

Thomas helps bring in little wooden stools.

Everyone sits down.

This is the moment they have **been** waiting for.

The teacher brings in a blackboard.

On it she writes a letter.

"A!" says the teacher.

"A!" says Thomas with the other children.

The teacher writes the letter with big strokes in the air.

The students do the same, over and over.

"Wonderful," says the teacher.

She hands out notebooks and pencils.

"Page one," says the teacher. Thomas opens his notebook to the first page and holds his pencil ready and waiting.

"Now write the letter A. Beautiful!" says the teacher as she looks at the students' work.

Every day Thomas learns something new.

Every day the teacher cheers him and the other children on. "Excellent job," she says. "Perfect, my learning friends!"

The nine **months** of the school **year** fly by.

The last day has come. The students' minds are fat with knowledge. **Their** notebooks are rumpled from learning.

Thomas and the other children call out, "Thank you, Teacher."

She smiles and says, "Well done, my hard-working friends! See you next year."

Thomas and the other children race home.

The school is empty, and just in time.
The big rains have started.
The drops come down hard and fast.

Strong winds tear at the grass roof.
The rain finds its way inside.
The school's mud walls are soaked and start to slump.
The mud desks, too.

Slowly, the school disappears until there is almost nothing left.

It doesn't matter. The letters have been learned and the knowledge taken away by the children.

Come September, school will start over. Thomas will be a big brother then, leading the children on their first day to school. They will all stand in front of their smiling teachers, ready to build their school again.

Meet James Rumford

James Rumford says, "I have made books since I was a little boy. I drew the pictures and wrote the words. I still like doing that."

James has always loved to travel and see new places. At one time, he lived in Africa. The ideas for his books and illustrations come from the places he has been and the people he has met. Today, James lives in Hawaii.

Author's Purpose

James Rumford wanted to write about how the yearly rains affected the children of Chad. Draw a picture of yourself doing something outdoors. Write what the weather is like.

C. Rumford

356

Respond to the Text

Retell

Use your own words to retell *Rain School.* The information on your chart can help.

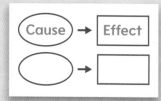

Write

What do the children in Rain School learn from their first lesson? Use these sentence starters:

Everyone worked...
The children learn...

Make Connections
COLLABORATE

How does the weather in *Rain School* affect the children? ESSENTIAL QUESTION

Compare Texts

Read about how rain affects some people and places.

Rainy Weather

Weather changes from day to day. Some days are sunny, and some days are rainy. When it rains, do you wish the rain would go away? You might, but we need rain.

How Rain Helps

All living things need water. Rain helps plants grow, so that people and animals have food. Rain falls on ponds, lakes, and rivers. Then animals can drink water all year long. People need water to drink, too. We also use it for cooking and cleaning.

Stormy Weather

We need rain, but rain can mean **storms,** and storms can mean problems. In a thunderstorm, thunder crashes! Lightning flashes! Lightning can strike trees or buildings.

A hurricane is a bigger storm. Heavy rains can cause a lot of **damage**. Winds can blow so hard that trees bend and break. There may be a flood. When it's over, people help each other clean it up.

Ready and Safe

Weather people can **predict** if a storm is on the way. Then we can stay safe.

In a thunderstorm or hurricane, the best place to be is inside. People may buy extra food, drinking water, and flashlights. Then they do not have to go outside. Soon the sun will be out. And then there will come another rainy day.

The red and yellow on this map show a storm.

Make Connections

How did the rain affect people in *Rain School*?
Essential Question

(bkgd) Ryan McVay/Lifesize/Getty Images; (inset) NOAA

Essential Question

What traditions do you know about?

Read about a family tradition that helps a girl make friends.

Go Digital!

Lissy's Friends

by Grace Lin

Lissy was the new girl at school.

Nobody talked to her.

Nobody smiled at her.

At the playground, Lissy stood on the merry-go-round by herself.

Because Lissy ate lunch alone, she was
finished **before** lunchtime was over. Since she
didn't have anything else to do, Lissy took the
lunch menu in **front** of her and began to fold it.
Soon, she had made a little paper crane.

"Hello," Lissy said to the paper crane. "I will call you Menu, and you will be my friend."

And to her surprise, Menu opened its eyes and blinked at her. Menu looked to the right, then to the left, and fluttered up with its paper wings.

367

The rest of the day, Lissy smiled a secret smile.

"Did you make any friends in school today?" Mommy asked when Lissy came home.

"Well," Lissy said, patting Menu in her pocket, "I did make one friend."

"Good," Mommy said. "I'm sure you'll make more **tomorrow**."

And she did. The next day, Lissy made lots of friends.

373

Her friends went with her ...

everywhere.

And Lissy was never alone.

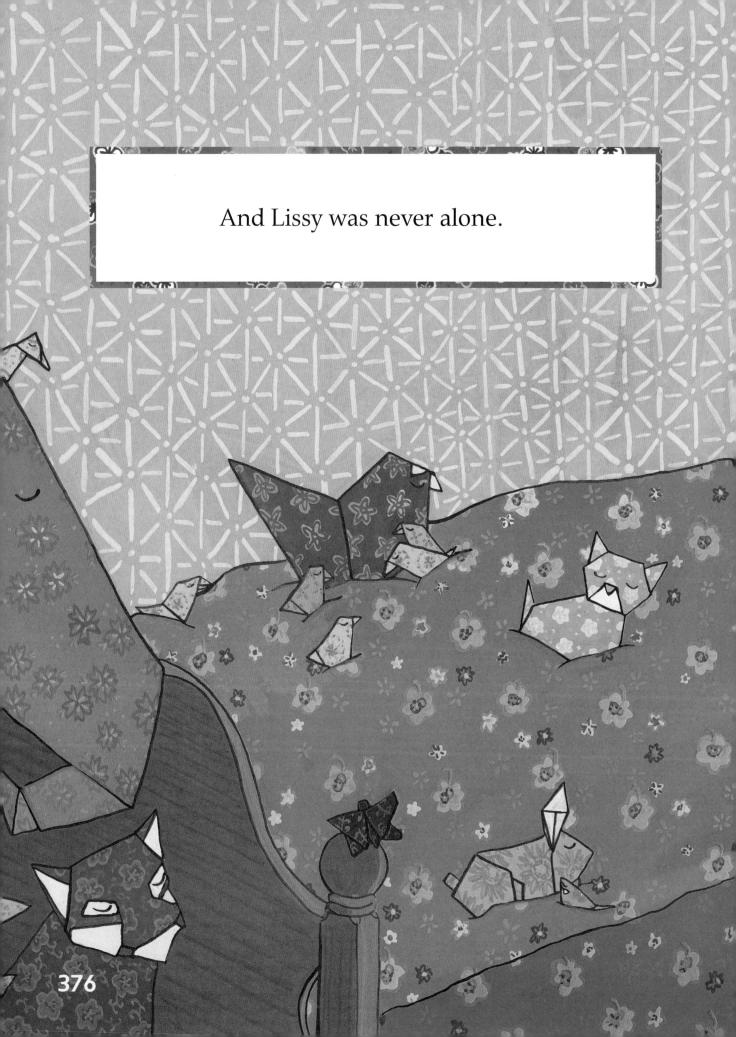

One day, Lissy **heard** a group of kids laughing as they went down the street. They stopped at one house and then another, but they didn't stop at Lissy's.

"Lissy," Mommy called from downstairs, "why don't you go with **your** friends to the playground? I think they are all headed that way."

Lissy looked at her paper friends.

"Yes," she said. "Let's go to the playground."

Lissy led her friends down the street and to the playground.

"We'll ride the merry-go-round first," she told them. "Then we can all ride together."

So all the paper animals crowded onto the merry-go-round, and Lissy began to **push** it. Round and round Lissy pushed. She ran so hard she didn't see that her friends were having a **difficult** time staying on ...

SWOOSH! The paper giraffe flew!
Then the paper elephant and the rabbit!
A strong wind caught them and carried
them up into the sky.

When Lissy jumped on, the merry-go-round was empty! She looked up and saw her paper friends flying away.

"No! Come back!" Lissy cried.

But they couldn't.

"No more friends," Lissy said, and she sat down on the merry-go-round and covered her face with her hands.

"Hey, is this yours?" a voice said.

Lissy looked up. There was a girl holding a paper crane. Menu!

"It's neat," the girl said. "Did you make it?"

Lissy looked at the girl. She was smiling at her. Lissy nodded.

"Can you show me how?" the girl asked. "I'm Paige."

Paige came over to Lissy's house, and Lissy showed her how to make a paper crane. Then they made a paper fox and dragonfly. They talked and laughed.

389

And the next day, Paige pushed Lissy on the
merry-go-round with lots and lots of friends.

Dear Lissy,

We hope you are doing well. We are having fun traveling the **world**. We miss you!

♡
your friends

P.s. Tell Menu Hello!

Lissy Lin
58 Paper Place
Valley Fold, MA
10000

Dear Lissy,

We hope you are doing
well. We are having fun
traveling the world. We
miss you!

♡
your friends

P.s Tell Menu Hello!

Lissy Lin
58 Paper Place
Valley Fold, MA
10000

Meet Grace Lin

When Grace was a child, she wanted to read books that made her feel like she belonged. So now, Grace writes books that encourage kids to be proud of their culture and that help readers appreciate Asian traditions. She likes to write the stories and make the art.

Author's Purpose

Grace Lin wanted to write about the tradition of making origami. Draw a picture of something that is a tradition in your family. Tell about your drawing.

Respond to the Text

Retell

Use your own words to retell *Lissy's Friends.*

Clue
↓
Clue
↓
Clue
↓
Theme

Write

Write a letter from Lissy to her paper friends telling them about how things are going now. Use these sentence starters:

Dear Paper Friends,...

Things are different now because...

Make Connections

COLLABORATE

What is a family tradition that you can share with others?
ESSENTIAL QUESTION

Making Paper Shapes

See the crane made out of folded paper? Folding paper to make different shapes is called **origami**. People in Asia have made origami for hundreds of years.

Kids learn this art from their mothers, fathers, and grandparents.

People in Japan make **decorations** for special days. One **holiday** is the Star Festival. Children sing songs and get treats to eat.

Families hang bright origami and slips of paper. Kids can write wishes on the slips and hang them from sticks. They hope their wishes come true.

You can make origami, too. Use these directions to turn a square of paper into a cute dog.

1. Start with a square of paper. Fold it down in half so it forms a triangle.

2. Fold it in half again, like this. Press down the edge to make a crease.

3. Open the paper so you see a crease in the center.

4. Start from the crease and fold down both sides of the paper to make ears. See the dotted line? It shows you where to fold.

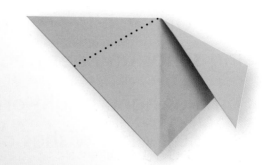

5. Now your dog will look like this.

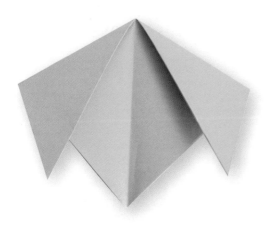

6. Fold back the top of your dog so it is flat. Fold back the bottom so it is flat, too.

7. You made a dog! Now you can draw a face on it.

Make Connections

What might Lissy do with this dog? **Essential Question**

Essential Question
Why do we celebrate holidays?
Read about how our country began.

Go Digital!

Happy Birthday, U.S.A.!

Why do we celebrate the Fourth of July?

Whiz! Boom! Bang!
That's the sound of fireworks that tear through the air. Colors light up the sky. Bands play and crowds roar. It's the Fourth of July!

Each year, people celebrate the birthday of the United States. It is a day for us all to share. We enjoy **favorite** things such as fireworks, parades, and picnics. This kind of party has **gone** on for over two hundred years. But how did this holiday begin?

Parades are a favorite way to celebrate July 4th.

In 1775, our **nation** was small. It had just
13 colonies. A colony is like a state, but
ruled by a leader far away. This ruler was
the king of England. The people in the
colonies did not like this. They felt the
king's rules were not fair. They felt he did
not care if they were happy.

Our country began
over 200 years ago.

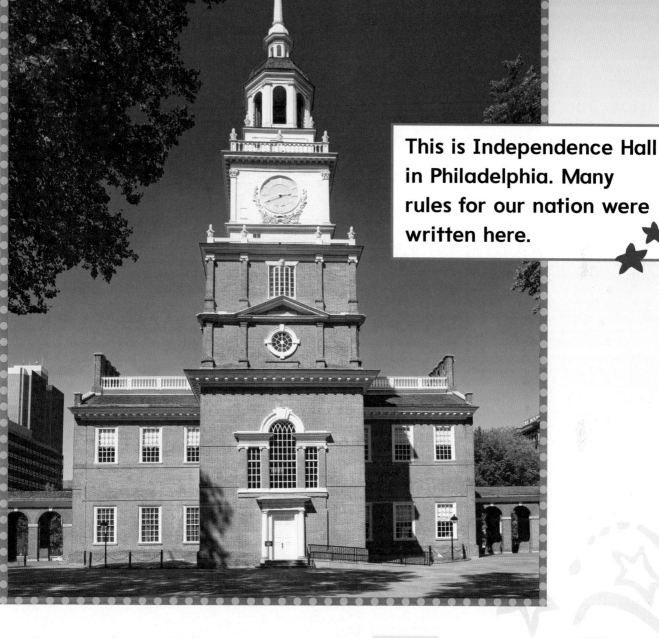

This is Independence Hall in Philadelphia. Many rules for our nation were written here.

On June 11, 1776, leaders of the **young** colonies met as a group called Congress. The people of the colonies wanted to split away from England. And the leaders wanted to **unite** to make new rules and write their own laws.

Thomas Jefferson led the team that wrote the Declaration of Independence. They wrote it in just a **few** weeks! It declares that people should be free to be happy and that they should be free from rulers far away. The writers wanted to choose their own kind of government.

Thomas Jefferson wrote the Declaration of Independence. Years later, he became the third president of the United States.

TIME FOR KIDS®

Thomas Jefferson and other leaders in Congress talked about how to split away from England.

Leaders started to sign the Declaration of Independence on July 4, 1776. They sent it to the king of England. He was **surprised** the colonies dared to do this. He did not want the colonies to be free.

The Declaration of Independence was first read out loud on July 4. Music blared and bells rang. One year later, fireworks lit up the sky on July 4.

This was just the beginning. It was a long fight for everyone in our nation to get freedom. But it would not have happened without the Declaration of Independence.

This is the Declaration of Independence. It told King George that the 13 colonies wanted to be free from England.

We celebrate our freedom and the declaration every year on the 4th of July. It's no **wonder** it is our nation's favorite holiday!

Respond to the Text

I. Use detail from the selection to retell. RETELL

2. What is the most important part of the Fourth of July? Why do you think so? WRITE

? 3. Why do we celebrate the Fourth of July? TEXT TO WORLD

Compare Texts

Read about how the 13 colonies grew to become the United States.

A Young Nation GROWS

In 1776, our nation had just 13 colonies. More than 2 million people lived here. Each colony later became a state. Look at the map of the colonies. Read the colony names below. Do you see any names you know?

Philadelphia

1776 Colonies

The 13 Original Colonies

1 Massachusetts
2 New Hampshire
3 New York
4 Connecticut

5 Rhode Island
6 Pennsylvania
7 New Jersey
8 Maryland

9 Delaware
10 Virginia
11 North Carolina
12 South Carolina
13 Georgia

Illustration: Beth Griffis Johnson

Today, our nation has 50 states. More than 320 million people live here!

Did you know that Philadelphia was our nation's first capital?

What is our nation's capital today? If you guessed Washington, DC, you are correct! It became the capital in 1790.

The United States Today

Philadelphia

Washington, DC

Make Connections

 What can you learn about the colonies from the map? **Essential Question**

Glossary

What is a Glossary? A glossary can help you find the meanings of words. The words are listed in alphabetical order. You can look up a word and read it in a sentence.

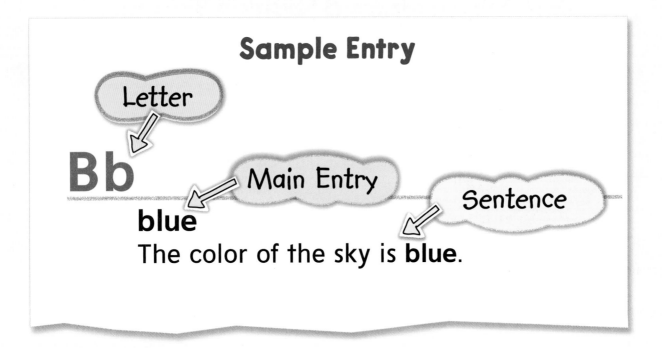

Sample Entry

Letter

Bb

Main Entry

Sentence

blue
The color of the sky is **blue**.

Aa

about
She likes to talk **about** her pet dog.

above
I saw the bird fly **above** the trees.

accept
Cal was happy to **accept** the gift.

animal
My favorite farm **animal** is a cow.

another
May I have **another** glass of water?

answer
Her **answer** to the question was yes.

Bb

balance
It is hard to **balance** on only one foot.

beautiful
The red flowers look **beautiful**.

because
Ty went to bed **because** he was tired.

been

I have never **been** on a plane.

before

Brush your teeth **before** you go to bed.

began

Our trip **began** on the bus.

better

Kim likes apples **better** than ice cream.

blue

The color of the sky is **blue**.

brother

I share a room with my older **brother**.

brought

Anna **brought** her lunch to school.

build

Jin likes to **build** things with blocks.

busy

Many cars drove on the **busy** road.

Cc

carry
Hope had to **carry** books to her classroom.

caught
I **caught** the ball in my baseball glove.

children
The **children** waved good-bye to their mom.

clever
The **clever** fox tricked the crow.

climb
Some cats like to **climb** up trees.

color
The **color** of my new dress is blue.

country
My friend moved to another **country**.

Dd

danger
A hot stove is a **danger** to a child.

demand

I **demand** that you return my pencil.

difficult

The problem was **difficult** to solve.

door

I lock the **door** when I leave the house.

Ee

early

Rosa wakes up **early** in the morning.

eight

All spiders have **eight** legs.

emergency

In an **emergency**, ask your parents for help.

enough

Sam had **enough** grapes, so he gave some to me.

eyes

I wear glasses to help my **eyes** see better.

Ff

fall

Cole saw the leaf **fall** from the tree.

fancy

The **fancy** house had many rooms.

father

My **father** walks me to school.

favorite

The dog's **favorite** toy is the red ball.

few

There are only a **few** pages left in the book.

find

Can you help me **find** my missing pencil?

flew

The plane **flew** high above the city.

food

I ate enough **food** for dinner.

found

Gwen **found** her socks in her shoes.

four
The kitten landed on all **four** of its legs.

friend
Brad asked his **friend** Emma to help him.

front
May I stand in the **front** of the line?

full
Rae's mom picked a lot of apples so her basket is **full**.

Gg

gathers
The blue jay **gathers** twigs for a nest.

give
I will **give** you a gift for your birthday.

gone
Ben has **gone** to his bedroom to sleep.

great
Nisha felt **great** after winning the race.

guess
Can you **guess** how many beans are in the jar?

Hh

hard
We studied **hard** for the test.

heard
We **heard** the bell and went into school.

Ii

idea
I will think of an **idea** for a new story.

instead
Will wants to read **instead** of play ball.

into
Joy watched the ducks dive **into** the lake.

Kk

knew
My mother **knew** how to get to the park.

know
I **know** that some sharks can swim quickly.

Ll

large

My dad's shoes were too **large** for my feet.

laugh

Jeb makes me **laugh** when he tells funny jokes.

leaped

The frog **leaped** into the pond.

learn

When I read books, I **learn** new words.

listen

Emily likes to **listen** to music.

love

I **love** my family because they take care of me.

Mm

money

Cass saved her **money** to buy new markers.

month

March is the **month** that comes before April.

more

A bucket holds **more** water than a cup.

mother

Her **mother** took care of her when she was ill.

Nn

nation

My friend comes from the **nation** of Mexico.

near

I sat **near** the sea to listen to the waves.

nobody

I rang the bell, but **nobody** was home.

none

None of the stores are open at night.

nothing

The empty box had **nothing** inside of it.

Oo

often

We went swimming **often** this summer.

oh

Oh! I didn't see you come in.

only

Ari wore the **only** coat he owned.

or

The family can have pasta **or** fish for dinner.

other

Nate likes this game more than the **other** one.

our

We gave **our** papers to the teacher.

over

A flock of birds flew **over** our heads.

Pp

partner

I asked Anya to be my **partner** for the game.

picture
Ray drew a **picture** with his pencil.

poor
The **poor** kitten lost its toy ball.

push
Paige had to **push** hard to open
the door.

put
Please **put** the plates on the table.

Qq

question
My mom told me the answer to my
question.

Rr

right
I know the **right** way to go home
from school.

round
The **round** orange rolled off the table.

Ss

scrambled
The squirrel quickly **scrambled** down the tree.

search
They had to **search** for the missing keys.

section
I planted corn in one **section** of the garden.

seek
Snakes **seek** the sun to get warm.

signal
My coach gave a **signal** to start.

small
The **small** ladybug walked on the leaf.

special
My birthday is a **special** day for me.

splendid
Having a playdate is a **splendid** idea.

start
Start the race when you hear the whistle.

stretched
I **stretched** my arm to reach the top shelf.

suddenly
I awoke **suddenly** when I heard the loud noise.

sure
Are you **sure** that you want that one?

surprise
The party for my sister was a **surprise**.

Tt

their
The players had **their** team photo taken.

thought
I **thought** about the book after I read it.

through
The train went **through** the tunnel.

tomorrow

It is sunny today, but it will rain **tomorrow**.

toward

The puppy ran **toward** the house.

trouble

The class was in **trouble** for talking too much.

Uu

unite

Our team had to **unite** to beat the other team.

unusual

The cat had an **unusual** pattern on its fur.

Ww

warm

The baby had a bath in **warm** water.

were

We **were** at home all day.

whole
There were eight slices of pizza in the **whole** pie.

woman
The **woman** carried her baby in her arms.

wonder
I **wonder** how many stars are in the sky.

would
Tomás **would** like to be in the play.

write
I **write** my name at the top of the paper.

Yy

year
There are twelve months in a **year**.

young
The **young** girl held her father's hand.

your
We can walk to **your** house.